Affirmations. Encouragement. Motivation.

WHAT
DID YOU SAY?

Statements for Daily Self—Talk

Affirmations. Encouragement. Motivation.

WHAT
DID YOU SAY?

Statements for Daily Self—Talk

Affirmations. Encouragement. Motivation.

Onedia Nicole Gage, Ph. D., CLC

Affirmations. Encouragement. Motivation.

Other Books by
Onedia N. Gage, Ph. D.

Are You Ready for 9th Grade . . . Again? A Family's Guide to Success
As We Grow Together Daily Devotional for Expectant Couples
As We Grow Together Prayer Journal for Expectant Couples
As We Grow Together Bible Study: Her Workbook
As We Grow Together Bible Study: His Workbook
The Best 40 Days of My Life: A Journey of Spiritual Renewal
The Blue Print: Poetry for the Soul
From Fat to Fit in 90 Days: A Fitness Journal
From Two to One: The Notebook for the Christian Couple
Hannah's Voice: Powerful Lessons in Prayer
The Heart of a Woman: The Depth of Her Spirit
Her Story The Legacy of Her Fight: The Bible Study
Her Story The Legacy of Her Fight: The Devotional
Her Story The Legacy of Her Fight: The Legacy Journal
Her Story The Legacy of Her Fight: Prayers and Journal
I Am.: 90 Days of Powerful Words: Affirmation and Advice for Girls
ILY! A Mother Daughter Relationship Workbook
In Her Own Words: Notebook for the Christian Woman
In 90 Days: What Will You Do?
In Purple Ink: Poetry for the Spirit
In Your Hands: A Dad's Impact on Your Daughter's Self-Esteem
Intensive Couples Retreat: Her Workbook
Intensive Couples Retreat: His Workbook
Living A Whole Life: Sermons Which Prompt, Provoke and Provide Life
Love Letters to God from a Teenage Girl
The Measure of a Woman: The Details of Her Soul
The Notebook: For Me, About Me, By Me
The Notebook for the Christian Teen
On This Journey Daily Devotional for Young People
On This Journey Prayer Journal for Young People
On This Journey Prayer Journal for Young People, Vol. 2
One Day More Than We Deserve Prayer Journal for the Growing Christian
Promises, Promises: A Novel
Queen in the Making: 30 Week Bible Study for Teen Girls
Queen in the Making: 30 Week Bible Study for Teen Girls Leader's Guide
There's a Queen Within: Her Journey to Self—Worth
She Spoke Volumes . . . And Then Some
Six Months of Solitude: The Sanctity of Singleness Notebook
Six Months of Solitude: The Sanctity of Singleness Prayers and Journal
Tools for These Times: Timely Sermons for Uncertain Times
With An Anointed Voice: The Power of Prayer

Affirmations. Encouragement. Motivation.

A Woman Like Me: A Bible Study
A Woman Like Me: A Daily Devotional
A Woman Like Me: A Sermonic Study
Yielded and Submitted: A Woman's Journey for a Life Dedicated to God
Yielded and Submitted: A Woman's Journey for a Life Dedicated to God—An
Intimate Study
Yielded and Submitted: A Woman's Journey for a Life Dedicated to God—
Prayers and Journal

The Nehemiah Character Series

Nehemiah and His Basketball
Nehemiah and His Big Sister
Nehemiah and His Bike
Nehemiah and His Flag Football Team
Nehemiah and His Football
Nehemiah and His Golf Clubs
Nehemiah and Math
Nehemiah and the Bully
Nehemiah and the Busy Day
Nehemiah and the Class Field Trip
Nehemiah and the Substitute for the Substitute
Nehemiah Can Swim
Nehemiah Found the Mud
Nehemiah Reads to Mommy
Nehemiah Writes Just Like Mommy
Nehemiah, the Hot Dog, and the Broccoli
Nehemiah's Family Vacation
Nehemiah's Favorite Teacher Returns to School
Nehemiah's First Day of School
Nehemiah's Sister Moved
Nehemiah's Visit to the Hospital

Dedication

For the Dreamer

For the Start—Up Entrepreneur

For the Start—Over Entrepreneur

For the Stagnant Entrepreneur

For the Successful Entrepreneur

Affirmations. Encouragement. Motivation.

Library of Congress

What Did You Say?

Affirmations. Encouragement. Motivation.

Purple Ink, Inc. Press
For Information address:
Purple Ink, Inc
10223 Broadway St., Ste. P292
Houston, TX 77584
www.purpleink.net ♦ www.onediagage.com

onediagage@purpleink.net ♦ onediagage@onediagage.com

ISBN:

978-1-939119-20-9
Printed in United States

What God Has to Say

Come unto me, all ye that labour and are heavy laden, and I will give you rest.

Matthew 11:28 (KJV)

For where your treasure is, there your heart will be also.

Matthew 6:21

[16] I pray that out of his glorious riches he may strengthen you with power through his Spirit in your inner being, [17] so that Christ may dwell in your hearts through faith. And I pray that you, being rooted and established in love, [18] may have power, together with all the Lord's holy people, to grasp how wide and long and high and deep is the love of Christ,

Ephesians 3:16—18

Affirmations. Encouragement. Motivation.

The Author's Message

Dear Business Owner/Dreamer:

What Did You Say? Is based on what people ask me all of the time: what did you just say? I am usually teaching or sharing something that is profound and we need to hear that again.

This time you will see it and apply it immediately. I have several life philosophies: 1) If not me, who? If not now, when? 2) What have you done today to invest in your future? 3) Put on your own air mask first. And, 4) What can I get done by Friday?

These philosophies get me through each day. The mechanism to achievement is what will do to propel yourself forward.

Find yourself in these pages. Be present in this moment. I know that is a tall ask, however, please get your focus on the task so that you can reach the goal that you have set for yourself.

If you need to seek my advice, please contact me onediagage@onediagagespeaks.com.

Otherwise, I will see you at the top!

Onedia Gage, Ph. D., CLC

Affirmations. Encouragement. Motivation.

The
Sayings

Affirmations. Encouragement. Motivation.

If not me, who?

If not now, when?

Today, I will _____

_____

_____

_____

_____

_____

_____

What will you do today to propel yourself forward?

Today, I will _____

_____

_____

_____

_____

_____

_____

STOP

PROCRASTINATING!

Today, I will _____

_____

_____

_____

_____

_____

_____

_____

STOP

PROCRASTINATING!

START

WORKING!

Today, I will _____

_____

_____

_____

_____

_____

_____

_____

The person in the room with the least to lose is the most powerful person.

Today, I will _____

_____

_____

_____

_____

_____

_____

Go Big!

Today, I will _____

_____

_____

_____

_____

_____

_____

Today, I will _____

_____

_____

_____

_____

_____

_____

_____

Do it big!

Do it now!

Do it afraid!

Today, I will _____

_____

_____

_____

_____

_____

_____

STOP THE SELF–SABOTAGE!

Today, I will _____

_____

_____

_____

_____

_____

_____

_____

Stop the self—doubt!

Today, I will _____

_____

_____

_____

_____

_____

_____

Read aloud:

"I believe in me!"

Now, say it like you actually believe it.

Today, I will _____

_____

_____

_____

_____

_____

_____

Today, I will _____

_____

_____

_____

_____

_____

_____

ACT LIKE YOU BELIEVE IN YOURSELF.

PEOPLE NEED TO FEEL IT.

YOU NEED TO SEE IT.

Today, I will _____

_____

_____

_____

_____

_____

_____

Today, I will _____

_____

_____

_____

_____

_____

_____

If you can't act like you believe in you, then act like you should because I believe in you.

Today, I will _____

_____

_____

_____

_____

_____

_____

Smile.

Today, I will _____

_____

_____

_____

_____

_____

_____

_____

Laugh.

Today, I will _____

_____

_____

_____

_____

_____

_____

Forgive yourself.

Today, I will _____

_____

_____

_____

_____

_____

_____

_____

PICK YOUR CHIN UP OFF OF YOUR CHEST.

Today, I will _____

_____

_____

_____

_____

_____

_____

Today, I will _____

_____

_____

_____

_____

_____

_____

Speak
success
into
existence.

Today, I will _____

_____

_____

_____

_____

_____

_____

You
deserve
to
win.

Today, I will _____

_____

_____

_____

_____

_____

_____

YOU

ARE

SPECIAL.

Today, I will _____

_____

_____

_____

_____

_____

_____

You
are
successful.

Today, I will _____

_____

_____

_____

_____

_____

_____

You are more than a conqueror.

Today, I will _____

_____

_____

_____

_____

_____

_____

LOVE.

Today, I will _____

_____

_____

_____

_____

_____

_____

Leap!

Today, I will _____

_____

_____

_____

_____

_____

_____

_____

Today, I will _____

_____

_____

_____

_____

_____

_____

Focus!

Today, I will _____

_____

_____

_____

_____

_____

_____

Focus!
Focus!
Focus!

Today, I will _____

_____

_____

_____

_____

_____

_____

_____

Get

out of

your

own way!

Today, I will _____

_____

_____

_____

_____

_____

_____

Make a decision.
Stick to it.
Take action.

Today, I will _____

_____

_____

_____

_____

_____

_____

_____

Be your best self.

If you don't know who that is, then call someone who does.

If you don't know that someone, then call me.

Today, I will _____

_____

_____

_____

_____

_____

_____

_____

Today, I will _____

_____

_____

_____

_____

_____

_____

Don't quit.

Don't ever give up.

Today, I will _____

_____

_____

_____

_____

_____

_____

Listen to your motivational song when you feel like quitting.

Today, I will _____

_____

_____

_____

_____

_____

_____

Do it because you love it!

Today, I will _____

_____

_____

_____

_____

_____

_____

DO IT BECAUSE YOU ARE GOOD AT IT!

Today, I will _____

_____

_____

_____

_____

_____

_____

_____

Do what sets you free.

Today, I will _____

_____

_____

_____

_____

_____

_____

_____

Do IT with your heart.
If you can't, then change directions immediately.

Today, I will _____

_____

_____

_____

_____

_____

_____

Do you recall when you were at your best self?

What does it take to return to that person?

By doing what?

By when?

Today, I will _____

_____

_____

_____

_____

_____

_____

_____

YOU ARE EVER–EVOLVING.

TAKE YOUR TIME TO ABSORB, RETAIN, AND PRACTICE WHAT YOU ARE TAKING IN.

Today, I will _____

_____

_____

_____

_____

_____

_____

Who is your mentor?

That is a trusted advisor, with whom you can be authentic and transparent so that you can grow. When will you find one? When will you engage him/her?

Today, I will _____

_____

_____

_____

_____

_____

_____

_____

Affirmations. Encouragement. Motivation.

Today, I will _____

_____

_____

_____

_____

_____

_____

_____

I will grow today.

Repeat this until you can believe it.

Today, I will _____

_____

_____

_____

_____

_____

_____

_____

I will lead today.

Repeat this until you understand the impact of your words.

Today, I will _____

_____

_____

_____

_____

_____

_____

I will give today.

Repeat this until you understand the benefit of your words.

Today, I will _____

_____

_____

_____

_____

_____

_____

I will do what is best for me and my goals.

Repeat this until you understand your role in achieving your goals.

Today, I will _____

_____

_____

_____

_____

_____

_____

Today, I will _____

_____

_____

_____

_____

_____

_____

Today, I will put my own air mask on first.

Today, I will _____

_____

_____

_____

_____

_____

_____

Breathe.

Today, I will _____

_____

_____

_____

_____

_____

_____

_____

Today, I will _____

_____

_____

_____

_____

_____

_____

Trouble don't last always.

Today, I will _____

_____

_____

_____

_____

_____

_____

RELAX.

Today, I will _____

_____

_____

_____

_____

_____

_____

This too shall pass.

Today, I will _____

_____

_____

_____

_____

_____

_____

Find the applause app and use it often.

Today, I will _____

_____

_____

_____

_____

_____

_____

YOU
ARE
GREAT!

Today, I will _____

_____

_____

_____

_____

_____

_____

You are amazing!

Today, I will _____

_____

_____

_____

_____

_____

_____

_____

You

are a

decision

maker.

Today, I will _____

_____

_____

_____

_____

_____

_____

YOU ARE A PROBLEM SOLVER.

Today, I will _____

_____

_____

_____

_____

_____

_____

Today, I will _____

_____

_____

_____

_____

_____

_____

You are designed to produce.

Today, I will _____

_____

_____

_____

_____

_____

_____

_____

You are determined to succeed.

Today, I will _____

_____

_____

_____

_____

_____

_____

Your work ethic will lead you to achievement.

Today, I will _____

_____

_____

_____

_____

_____

_____

Make today
the best day
of your life.

Today, I will _____

_____

_____

_____

_____

_____

_____

Invest in your business education.

Take a class.

Read a book.

Today, I will _____

_____

_____

_____

_____

_____

_____

Think about solutions when you consider your problems.

Today, I will _____

_____

_____

_____

_____

_____

_____

WHO IS YOUR COACH?

WHEN WILL YOU FIND AND SECURE ONE?

Today, I will _____

_____

_____

_____

_____

_____

_____

_____

Today, I will _____

_____

_____

_____

_____

_____

_____

What do you do to study your craft?

Today, I will _____

_____

_____

_____

_____

_____

_____

Live your biggest dreams today!

Today, I will _____

_____

_____

_____

_____

_____

_____

Live your best life today!

Today, I will _____

_____

_____

_____

_____

_____

_____

Don't stand in your own way!

Today, I will _____

_____

_____

_____

_____

_____

_____

What is really standing in your way?

What can you do to move that obstacle?

Today, I will _____

_____

_____

_____

_____

_____

_____

_____

Today, I will _____

_____

_____

_____

_____

_____

_____

Rest.

Get a good night's sleep.

Every night.

Today, I will _____

_____

_____

_____

_____

_____

_____

TAKE CARE OF YOUR HEALTH.

WHEN WAS THE LAST TIME YOU HAD A HEALTH CARE CHECKUP?

GET REGULAR ANNUAL CHECK—UPS.

Today, I will _____

_____

_____

_____

_____

_____

_____

Believe.

Today, I will _____

_____

_____

_____

_____

_____

_____

Drink water.

Today, I will _____

_____

_____

_____

_____

_____

_____

Exercise.

Today, I will _____

_____

_____

_____

_____

_____

_____

Establish a routine for eating, drinking water, and resting.

Today, I will _____

_____

_____

_____

_____

_____

_____

Establish legal entities and succession planning.

You will need a will.

Today, I will _____

_____

_____

_____

_____

_____

_____

Today, I will _____

_____

_____

_____

_____

_____

_____

Affirmations. Encouragement. Motivation.

ACKNOWLEDGEMENTS

God, thank You for Your plans for me. Thank You for *What Did You Say?* *Affirmations. Encouragement. Motivation.* and choosing me to complete Your project with the words that come out of my mouth. I just want to please You. Thank You for continuing to anoint me and to invest in me and my gifts, which keep surprising me. Thank You for loving and forgiving me.

Jordan and Nehemiah, thank you for supporting me and my endeavors. Thank you for loving me, especially when I do nothing without a pen and a clipboard, thank you for enduring my late nights, your ideas, the sounding board, the love, and the support. Thank you for celebrating our legacy.

To my prayer partners and to my accountability partners, thank you for the long talks, the powerful prayers, and the encouragement. To my pastor and church family, thank you so much for your love and support.

Affirmations. Encouragement. Motivation.

Onedia N. Gage speaks volumes. Sometimes no one is listening. Other times people cannot listen enough. But what she says is quite powerful. Timely. Judicious. Poignant. Insightful. Direct. Authentic. True.

Please feel free to contact and share your feedback. onediagage@onediagagespeaks.com, or @onediangage (twitter). www.onediagagespeaks.com Blogtalkradio.com/onediagage Youtube.com/onediagage10 Facebook.com/onedia-gage

Affirmations. Encouragement. Motivation.

CONFERENCE SPEAKER ♦ WORKSHOP LEADER

To invite Dr. Gage to speak at your event,

Please contact us at: www.onedigagespeaks.com

@onediangage (twitter) ♦ onediagage@onediagagespeaks.com ♦ facebook.com/onediagage

youtube.com/onediagage ♦ blogtalkradio.com/onediagage ♦ ongage (Instagram)

Affirmations. Encouragement. Motivation.

Publishing

Do you have a book you want to write, but do not know what to do?
Do you have a book you need to publish but do not know how to start?
Would publishing move your career forward?

Let us help
onediagage@purpleink.net ♦ www.purpleink.net
281.740.5143

Affirmations. Encouragement. Motivation.

www.ingramcontent.com/pod-product-compliance
Lightning Source LLC
Chambersburg PA
CBHW031902200326
41597CB00012B/515